Out Of The Corner
Of My Eye

Unheard Voices Of The Homeless

A Book of Prose, Poems and Sayings
By
Sue L. Adkins
Foreword by Henry O. Adkins

Sue L. Adkins

ISBN 0-9672605-9-0
Cheudi Publishing Plano, Texas 75094-0572

Table of Contents

Foreword by Henry O. Adkins
Special Thanks from Henry O. Adkins

THE DRINKING TREE
RAILROAD WORKER
WILL WORK FOR FOOD
THE DUSTY TRAIL
B.U.B.S (Bums Under Bridges)

Foreword
by
Henry O. Adkins

As Director of the City of Dallas Day Resource Center for the Homeless, I would go home to my wife, Sue after a day's work and talk about some of my experiences, challenges, and problems managing people caught up in a terrible plight. I shared with her the unusual and different world of the homeless. I worked five years with the population, and during that time heard and saw things I never would have imagined. I was exposed to a sad underworld, and got to see the situation close-up and observe how things operated. Most would find as I did, the behaviors and actions of those out on the streets of Dallas strange and abhorrent. Night living on the pavement was hard. Some inhabitants, not all, stayed in night shelters, which offered a semblance of safety. But large groups stayed out and slept on downtown sidewalks in the shadow of tall buildings. Most slept in front of the day center that was closed on evenings and weekends.

The Homeless population is a diverse group. Many there have fallen on hard times. Not all come to stay; and those who don't have upbeat and positive attitudes. They seldom dwell on what brought them there. Their focus is getting off the streets and moving on. It's hard to believe, but there are some who are out there by choice. And they love it. They claim the streets as their own and try hard to keep things like they are. They don't want it to change. Some even proclaim a love for the streets and that life. So many I worked with I still think about. There was one young man in particular I helped get a job. He would come and talk to me every morning before he went to work. His plan was to get his life back on track. Things went fine for almost three months. But one payday instead of coming by to talk, he went to the crack house. He stayed there five days and spent every penny of his paycheck. It was two weeks before he got back to my office again. He walked in and I was startled to see his condition. He looked horrible and smelled worse. He told me he hadn't slept much the past two weeks. He had lost weight, his job, and my trust. But he didn't seem to care. I talked to him about getting help from a free program he could go into that same day. That's when he looked at me and said that he loved cocaine and wished he had a mountain of the stuff. As we talked something or somebody outside my office door got his attention. He mumbled something about dope, and got up, left my office, rushing out to try and catch another high. I was disappointed and felt like he was not only letting himself down, but everybody who worked so hard to help him leave the streets. This guy was a college graduate and came from a professional family in the suburbs. He was a well spoken, intelligent man who had lost his way.

Two years past and I was moved into another position. One day he found me and strolled into my new office at City Hall. He was clean cut, and looked nice. He had gained weight and seemed so different from the last time I saw him. He was well dressed and clean shaven like some you see in ads on television. He told me he was a member of the Dallas International Street Church. A good friend, Karen Dudley was the founder and pastor of that ministry. As he talked about the church and its mission I could see that a real change had taken place in his life. He sparkled with excitement as he told me he no longer did drugs and he didn't miss it. He gave all the credit to GOD for his transformation. And I did as well. He raved about the work of the Church and Pastor Dudley. Now he had a different outlook on life and a purpose for living. How unfortunate that this young man was a minority among the homeless I knew.

Some do find their way off the streets but most do not. Some don't want to leave and others just give up. Downtown Dallas and other cities are full of long term street people. There are a number of B.U.B.s (Bums under Bridges) scattered throughout the urban scene. You see a few guys on corners with signs reading, "Will Work for Food;" or

"Viet Nam Veteran; Please Help." They are not going away. And more are coming. The Day Resource Center for the Homeless was always full. And every week there was a fresh new group added to its ranks. The numbers continue to grow. The homeless population is right in front of us all. They are out there, all around, where we can see them. They are not trying to hide. And they speak out with loud voices: "Here I am! Look at me! See me!" We do. I see them. My children would come by my office. They saw, spoke to, and treated them with respect. My kids saw the people I worked with and their circumstance. They saw how they lived and that some had problems. They saw people, nothing else. They were taught to treat all people with kindness and respect. But for some people the homeless are a huge scourge. They see homeless and look away off in the distance. The homeless see them rush pass and around, trying not to look, as they move away. Maybe that rare one who happens to see, says: "I am only able to tolerate the view by squinting and looking *Out of the corner of my eye.*" We need to look at them. We must acknowledge and try to help. They are not going away. No. They are here to stay.

My wife listened to me talk about my work and experiences. She wrote it all down. I hope these stories help give a close-up view so all can see and learn the plight of a growing segment in our community. With these stories we hope all will see the condition of the Homeless; and look in their faces so you won't have to tell others "I can only see them **"OUT OF THE CORNER OF MY EYE."**

Sue L. Adkins

Special Thanks

From Henry O. Adkins

A Special Thanks goes out to everyone who worked with me at the Dallas Homeless Day Resource Center. Without your help I could not have survived the struggle. Thank you. These are just a few of the many soldiers who fought the fight every day. And to the many others not named, you too have my gratitude.

Sue Reed (The Social Work profession's Social Worker)

Robert L. Hines (The Deep Ellum Poet)

Jeanette Lane (Phoenix Ministry, Who brought true love to the people)

Patrick Martin (Homeless Pastor and Prayer partner from the Potter's House)

Georgia Reese (Our church lady and administrator)

Carol Lester (My true friend and dedicated Prayer partner)

Karen Dudley (Pastor Dallas International Street Church and Prayer partner)

Vivian Pogue (Another true friend who always looked out for me)

Ronald Cowart (Where I go he goes and where he goes I go)

Steve Ladd (Blues D.J. and Advocate for the Homeless)

Michael Crawford (Calm, Rational, and Fair)

Karen Boudreaux (Will find the grant money)

Lamar Walton (Pastor/Encourager; The Kingdom Missionary Church)

Pat Makeil, (A Gathering of Willing Hands /committed to the cause)

Teresa Johnson (Following The Son every day)

Jacqueline Surles (Plano Shiloh Baptist Church brining hope to the hopeless)

Janet Draper (Plano Shiloh Baptist Church; a true Homeless warrior)

David Galvan (Pastor, New Life Baptist Church, Garland)

Edna Pemberton (Homeless Coalition; always improving the lives of others)

Clora Hogan (Endless Choices, publisher and editor telling the homeless everything is possible)

Desi Jackson (VA Homeless Healthcare a true soldier)

Sue L. Adkins

Out Of The Corner Of My Eye

They see us but they don't
Come to help the downtrodden
Dispossessed and troubled
We notice how they look at us
Out of the corner of their eyes
Won't view us straight on
Our situation may be contagious
Can't chance catching nothing
That would be outrageous.
To keep from passing it on
Rubber gloves are a must
Remarks in patronizing tones

"Don't stand, get too close
Try or hope to understand
These folks are crazy, unsafe
With looks strange and weird"
We're told they mean no harm
Though it's our suspicion
Most are void of ambition
And could do much better
They have our permission.
Many have storms, battles
Trials to weather, still they
Need to get it together.

It's sad how they look at us
Blame and judge our condition
Feel bad and say they're sorry
But loath, hate our miserable
And unfortunate position
Though we size them up too
And wonder ourselves if most

Not all, but more than a few
Don't they know the real
Reason they come is to
Rack up points with *Him*
Oh, but some have pure hearts
And never weigh the risks
Or point a finger of blame
They accept, do their part
Take responsibility, seek truth
And recognize we're the same
Then let it settle in their hearts.

Out of the corner of our eyes
Seeking no measure of fame
It takes so little, not much
One misstep, a poor decision
Or circumstance of birth
To make the difference
And change the picture
Who comes out on top

Out of the corner of my eye
Is the past and future
Can't purchase His mercy
With flawed motivation
"Do right by others"
Not expecting compensation
Open your heart, move ahead
With vigor, might and force
Out of the corner of our eyes
We accept what we can
Shield our minds from the
Bright glare of all the rest
To keep from turning off
Altogether or taking in
Too much all at once
It's a safety measure.
You deal with crisis
Build up solid treasure
Encourage mini successes
Try to escape the failures

You, me, we... all of us
Must not turn away, no
In time decide, know and say
I can take in only so much
Bits, tiny pieces from all I see
"Out of the corner of my eye..."

Slab Names

To remain right here or go away
Roaming city streets, towns
Or choose to stay
And claim a space
At the end of day
Lugging worlds of time
A tired weathered face
On to that stark
Far off distant place
Few linger, spend time and learn,
Recall a past, the scars they earn
Or choose to forget
Hidden thoughts of a dead past,
Long lists of crimes forgotten fast
Family ties, loads of sorrow

But only now matters

No cares for tomorrow.

Actions, looks, assign a name.

Few keep the one mom gave

At birth when they came

No bubba or junior.

Not a one I recall.

No Lil' Brother; Tay-tay, Junebug.

Instead there's Paul, Barry

Anthony, James and William

All labels given at birth

That binds to memory

Our mothers, Dads,

Uncles and Aunt

To Sisters, Brothers

And Cousins of worth

Recollections of home

Stored up and buried.

When needed, retrieved,

Used to brag, tell of small glories

Secret forgotten terrors
Deep hidden stories--
A renaming takes place
There out on the slab.
And the one you had
Won't stick, seldom lasts
A nickname you got called
All your life refuses to cling
Cause once you're pegged
No matter the reason
Struggle or strife
How you're viewed now
Says what's real.
Your past life's a mystery
Old titles for now sealed.

Tweedy

We call her Tweedy.
"Tweee-dee!"
Her light, tight, chirping voice
That quick, thin, possessed look.
An alert head jerks, turns
Her revolving eyes stretch
Opened wide, searching
Piercing, protruding, brooding,
Snatching a glimpse, snippets
Of things all around
Wanting to find one to care
And relate that part of
Her life she can share.
So far from home,
No wish to return to

Where it is she came from
Back to a time long lost
And that life unsung
Her past once uncovered
Fuels those in charge
So pleased to discover
And send her back to
That distance traveled
Through shadows from
A place she once knew
Back long ago for miles
Over roads, tracks
Dim memories of a
Place she's told was home
Back to family where
They say she belongs.
"Why be stuck with
Another city's problems
Send them all back
To be retrieved by

Hometowns far away and
Lessen the city's count.
Return them all to that
Place of their birth
Let them handle their own"
Reclaim castoffs and
Relieve crowded cities
Of their human burdens;"
At the end of her journey
She's greeted with kindness
An acceptance at first
She re-enters their lives
Carrying all she owns
In a huge stuffed satchel
And gigantic purse;
Now she was home.
None were sure why
Or when she left
Nor where she'd gone;
One day she was there

The next she was not

A vacancy unnoticed

That didn't leave a blot.

Some seemed glad to see her

And the others maybe not

Hugs, smiles, a few tears shed

Some insincere smirks

A simple prayer was lead.

Her return overtook them at first.

So much time had passed

Everything happened so fast

There's no need to pretend

The difference was vast.

She'd changed, to their dread.

That steady working girl

And striving good person was

Now this strange prodigal one; an

Avalanche of recollections surfaced

Revisited from beginning to end

Seeing her again brought a flood

And marathon of memories
Her mischievous crimes
Swelled in their heads
And convinced them
She was better off instead
Away in that far off place that
Shields - the blinds of borders
Soon a change from conjecture
To certainty and fact; they would
Send her right back to where
She had just come from
Away from their little town
Of gossip, eyes, and mess
No planned good-byes
Or need to wait.
All hurried, scraped funds
Together and returned
Her back without delay
Soon Tweedy had gone
And landed back just

The same on familiar turf
Most never knew she left.
Nothing about her changed.
In the fall of the year
The purge put on hold, ended
Filed away, no plans to try again
She was back, part of the place
The surroundings and space
No further attempts made to ship
Her or others off, and away
To a cloudy unwelcomed past
That's murky and gray. No.
She'd stay till forever in this place
Her recovered home and space.

WOLF

That's Wolf over there.

A body, long, thin coal black

He speaks in a noticeable

Heavy tone so deep and real

The guy slides up to you

Quiet as morning snow

Head bobbing

Tilted to one side

His face fixed in a

Menacing scowl

Looking for what's "owed" him

It's his "condition"

He's 'medical'

Keeps reminding you that

He's got "the poisoned blood."
And tries to use it
To his advantage
His mission: To figure out
"A way to get over on you
"Man I need a..." he says.
"Hey man! I'm HIV!
Got AIDs!
I'm gon die *anyway!*
What I got to lose...?"

Those around him
Know his story and
Tell him the truth.
"Stop *them* drugs man!"
They say.
"Why?" he says.
A mask of acceptance
Shields his pain
"Why should I?

I DO IT ALL!
I got nothing to loose!
I'm dying anyway man!" he says.
"Yeah, hey, we know!
We heard your story.
But they got places you can go!
You don't have to die out here!
They got 'bad blood' places!"
They want him to get it, understand.
"I know all about that!" he said.
"That's not for me!" He's yelling now.
"I'm gon' die anyway!
Got to die some place!
Won't matter where!
Naw! I'm not goin no-where!
But folks could give me
Some **respect** man!" he said.
"Hey! Give *yourself* some respect!
You got to want it!" they say.
Naw. He's not goin no place.

He'll stay right here,

That's a fact.

He'll be here till

The end comes.

And it will.

It'll come sooner

Then he knows.

SMOKEY

"Hey! Smokey!"

He's another one.

Man tryin' to kill his self

Usin' the two quickest ways

Drugs and Alcohol

Everybody tol' him

He needs to stop drinkin

Acts proud of his time

"Been out here thirteen years

And still young!

Thirty-five years old!" he says.

He looks a lot older.

Its sad cause this

Life's gon' finish him off.

He's been told,

Warned lots of times
"Huh! I'm already dead!"
He cracks a thin somber smile.
A man with a death wish
But few know why.
One guess is he can't see
His way back through a foggy
Memory of better times
All is cloudy around him
Out and back away from here.
But in this place he knows what's
Coming every day;
Who'll hassle him, who won't
What he can do, what he can't.
Who to mess with and ignore
Who's got what he wants
And who don't.
It's all clear 'round here.
No big push to work it out
And make it day-to-day.

TINY

Resolved to the hum-drum

Knows her role, plays the part

Never forgets her lines.

Says she's forty-five years old.

Could a' fooled me!

Calls herself "uh ole lady"

Always needing a quarter

Acts like it's a fifty dollar gold piece.

Made her-self believe

She can get anything with it.

Thinks if she can

Just get her that quarter

Everything will be fine.

So she keeps asking everybody

Till she gets one in her hand, and

Once she succeeds it's like the
World can start turning again.
"Ole lady needs to git somethin
Outta that vendin machine!
Got a quarter for uh ole lady?"
Stays in a welfare apartment
Signed up for a work program
So they got her a place to stay.
Almost got put out once
A man was living with her
Got whispered, talked about
And it got back to the one
That makes decision in lives
They told Tiny she couldn't
Have nobody dropping in
And living with her
She didn't see it that way.
"What you saying?
I got 'a have somebody!
I'm uh ole lady but I ain' dead!"

That's telling um Tiny.
Stand up for your rights.
You need somebody!
We all do.

THE RAYMONDS

That's the 'Raymonds
Hope they make it
Get off these streets
Been treading through
Thankless Colorless existence
And mounds of setbacks
That can hover and snare.
Problems envelope lives
Drugs batter and push
Bodies lined up against walls
Countless victims get pinned
Shot, put out of their misery
Few escape the barriers.
Worms of hopelessness bore
Tunnel through souls, the

Surprise is that any survive.

She's white, middle aged.

He's black, younger than her

But time can be cruel.

Both started out alone, lonely

Separate, poles apart. She

Had bouts of mental illness

Plus addiction to crack

She stumbled to the slab and

Was sleeping in a cardboard box

The Raymonds a sort of success

Story by the measure of some

He's a contractor with a super IQ.

Started but never finished college.

It seemed a waste of time to him.

What he did was work

For a big utility company

Got assigned to a crew and

Spent endless days running wire

Lining up, installing poles

And cross beams.
He did fine, made big money
Helped his family that
Latched on to him for
Help with rent and more.
But the tide changed.
And all of a sudden
Things turned around and
Flipped upside down
His company cut back
He lost his job and discovered
Just how alone he was.
Those he helped pushed him away
Became strangers silent to his pleas
"Can't help you," they said.
"Nothing we can do!"
Good he saved up.
He had $10,000.
He took it, left town, and
Found a new place where

All around were strangers,

Folks with no interest in him

What he had, his happiness

Or whether he was even alive

He was in the big city

Sitting in a club

Drinking, dancing, having

Fun meeting folks, hoping maybe to

Find somebody to share a little time.

It wasn't long before disaster struck.

He got robbed. So quick

He was broke, dejected and sad.

Everything was gone. All he had.

He got scared, and then mad. A

Fight broke out, they called the cops.

Everything got weird, fuzzy.

He discovered the loss right away

"Somebody got my money!

Hey! Somebody took it!

I had it right in here!

It was here when I come in!
Right here in this side pocket!"
He patted and poked where it had been
Reached in, grabbed the pocket
Snatched, pulling it out
Stretching the stitched pouch
To show it was empty.
He checked again for holes.
"I had it here! Lots a' money!
'Right in here!
Now it's gone!" he said.
"What? Hey Man!
What you saying! I took it?
That I did it?
You the one come in buyin' drinks
Actin' all friendly like!" they said.
"Yeah, but somebody got it!
I had a pocket full of money
When I got here and
Now it's gone!" he said.

"Well, wasn't me!" the guy said.

"It's got a' be one a you!"

"You come straight over and

Sit down right here at my table!

Give me my money man!"

The owner heard the commotion

And rushed on over to him

"Hey! Take it easy! Ain' havin

None a' that in here!

You gon have to leave!" he said.

"I ain' goin' nowhere

Widout my money!" he said.

"Look man, we done called the cops!

Cops been called!" he said.

"I ain' done nothin wrong!" he said.

Then he lost it, started swinging

Trying to get at the one

He was sure stole from him.

He yelled and pointed at the thief.

Right then the cops came in.

'

It was hard trying to explain.
He leaned in reaching, to point
Out the guilty one, but the police
Just wanted him to hush
Settle down and leave
He was surrounded, but he kept
Talking, raging; "That guy right
Over there stole my money!"
That's when his fist landed on
The jaw of one of them cops, and
They wrestled him to the floor
Put him in handcuffs
And drug him off to jail.
Stayed locked up eight months.
He got out and
Wandered the streets
Drinking, hanging around,
Got shooed away
Was told to move on
And he slept on the sidewalk.

That became his new home.

He wanted to disappear

Be ground into the asphalt, die.

That's when they found each other.

They went from the sidewalk

To a cardboard box, a tent, and

Into a Southside apartment

They're different from the others

Trying to straighten out their lives

They got started in a program

And both been working hard

They're real smart, got brains

Can talk about anything

Way over most folks heads.

They read two, three

Books or more a week

That's unusual out here.

They got family

Children, grandchildren

And big plans to get on course

Turns and detours come but
They know what they need to do.
The Raymonds can make it!
They got to.
If for no other reason
Than to prove it can be done.

BLACK   SNOW   BLUE

"BLACK"

Black" is just that, Black.

No need to wonder

Or try to analyze

That fact Mack

The man is Black

Smooth

A chocolate snack

All colors mixed together

Agitated to get the total effect

"Been this way all my life"

He explains without regret

"Use to think about it all the time

Did for quite a while," he said

His face set in a big smile.
"...didn't worry me
When I was little
Always felt like
That was just my name
And who I was
Don't know who tagged me
But whoever did
Must a' not been sorry
Since they never
Came back to apologize."

So that got to be his name
That's fine in the neighborhood
"Never entered my mind
To be no way but accepting
I'm 'Black' and that's that
Not a curse or blessing."

Friends and family

Savvy enough

To use the title only around

Certain ones, in familiar places

Never had to explain

On home ground

And within earshot

But the tide turned

That day in a space

At school when that

Name was said by one

Not on the approved list

And it brought the first

Of many fights when

Some spread the label

That came at a time in

Our History when words

Coming from the wrong

Lips could be dynamite

And would draw blood

That word when said
By the unauthorized
Started fights and he was
Not always the winner.
The depth of his hue
Never lent itself to magic
Strength or super power
But he made it through
And knew the place where
It was accepted
Without question or shame
Was no need to defend or
Excuse its implications.
"Hey Black!"
"Yeah man that's me!
What's up?"

SNOW

Snow's black too.
"Snow?
That your name?"
"Naw!"
"Why they call you that?"
"Cause I ain' that's why.
I'm not pure or white as
None a that
But call me Snow
And I answer.
OK?
Yeah
Whatever you say

BLUE

Blue's not dark as Black

No need to say more 'bout that

"Got no problem or conflict

That's all I know Jack

Don't bother me none

No need to rattle on

Cause I'm just me

This one you see

Now here's a clue

The name's the same

To everybody

"I'm Blue!"

THREE REDS

Over there's one of the Reds.

...The only one still out here.

Lighter by three shades

Than the other two

But darker than most except

Snow, Black and Blue

The Red that's still here is

Red number one

Once he got sent back to Ohio.

He wrestles with mental problems

That brings pain and sorrow.

He couldn't fight it

That time he hopped on the bus

Was headed off away from here
He set looking straight ahead
While it pulled out and on
Back to a before time and place
Where he had lived but left.
It was a far off past space
And he moved around
In, about, out, and on
To other towns, spheres
Before ending up right back here
With a mind that comes and goes
Now he's left with so little to give.
He like most came from a long way off
Troubled ones attract others and more
You watch them gather, huddle,
Cling. The numbers grow.
They stumble to this place
Where they get fed
Then on to the next
Handed a pair of shoes

A blanket, coat, and
Something to eat
Toiletries stuffed in a pack
Some wash where, when they can.
Most drink, fall into a stupor and
And never come to themselves
To retain and reclaim the clear mind
That's meant to last a lifetime.
Some use and misuse
Drugs and alcohol
But claim there's no problem.
It's not an enviable life.
They attract trouble
Day, night and
Many end up in a fix
A life surrounded by fear
Meanness, menace
A painful, conniving existence
Woven in deceptive spirits
Some use their wits to convince

Gain and maintain a following
With eyes shut to the real picture.
Few look out for another's good.
In a sea of mercenaries floating
Just above the conditions
Of those they pretend to help
Some feign friendship, interest
And offer the "mark" inclusion
Like that one sitting there
Away off from the gathering
At a distance
His mind dark and sad
From another time and place
Still the bottle is passed around
And handed over to him so now
It's his chance to take part
And like others in the place
He's dazed, spaced out
Not able to think, take
Or hold the bottle and drink.

Somebody wraps his hands
Around, pulls it up to his mouth
Helps him pass it on down the line
And then sends it back.
That's Red.

The other Red, Red Three
Got in a scrap, like always
Was taking a drink from a "forty,"
And started messing with folks
Like he sometimes did
But this time it brought big trouble.
All knew it was bound to happen
He'd do something dumb.
It wasn't like he had a
Prayer of surviving
You could feel it coming, and
Once it happened all you could do is
Cover your eyes with your arm,
Pray, send out sympathy

For the lick he was about to get

Right up side his head

BLAM!

He got clocked.

Just before he hit the slab

A stupid look of satisfaction

Came across his face

And he fall over flat.

FLOOPH!

There he lay undisturbed.

The last time was a bloody mess.

Red just wouldn't stay down!

"Lay down man!

LAY THE HELL DOWN,

YOU OLE FOOL! WUMP!"

Aw-w-w...!

I almost went over

And punched him myself

But I didn't.

Didn't have brains enough

To take the count
Cops came, shipped him off to jail
And we haven't seen him since.

SLAB OVERNIGHT

They start early

Sectioning off territory

Lots of couples marking

A space of privacy

For a peaceful night's rest

But sleep never comes fast.

"Hey! Mr. Man!"

Somebody calls to the overseer.

"Yeah!" he said, getting set

For whatever the night brought.

"Got me some chicken here

I'm gon need to eat

And I got a' smoke right after.

I need to get out a' the buildin

So I can do that?" He said.

"Naw! Uh-uh!" the man said.

"...ain't no in and out!

Once you come in

You stay for the night! So

Either you don't eat that chicken

Or you gon' have to go out

Eat it, smoke, and

Find some other place

To go, 'cause you

Not getting back in here.

It's all up to you," he said.

The tentative resident nodded that

He understood. Then he shrugged

"Yeah, but I sure do want

To eat this chicken," he said.
"Oh yeah, is that right?
Well, huh! You got yourself
A real dilemma, don't you?"
The director stood posed with a
Determined, stubborn; stern look.
"Yeah I have. 'Cause I sure do love
Fried chicken," the resident said.
He stood there weighing his options
Trying to think up something
That would help him maybe
Come up with a compromise.
He had to find a way to
Get around that spoken rule.
It meant waiting for the right
Opportunity to get what he wanted
He had a knack for getting over
Around and through most rules
And this night would be no different.
Things started out good. He'd had

His dinner and saw his chance
When more food was brought in, and
Bums left out in the weather begged
For sanctuary from the freezing night
That was his opportunity to slip out
Unnoticed, light a smoke
And enjoy it to the last.
When the back door opened
Again for more deliveries
He made a quick twisting move and
Slipped his shivering body back inside.
He was pleased with his cunning
And delighted by his slick manner
But he didn't go unnoticed.
His temporary jailer spied him as
He dragged his back foot inside just
Before the door slammed shut,
He got a strained look
But never a word was said.
The director's eyes left no doubt

That should he try it again
He would be acquainted with the
Elements for the rest of the night
There was no need for words.
Both understood the silence.
It was loud and clear.

BIG BABY

Her constant whine

Seemed right

They got use to

Hearing it over days

Months, years, at night

From that first

Time they saw her

The poor dear

Thought she was still

That cute, young, sweet,

Loveable, good looking, fine

Girl she once was when

Dudes flipped and morphed

Into irrational crazies

Seeing and watching
Her walk could turn them into
Blithering idiots, barking
And begging for abuse
Now her voice takes on
A stark urgency
She needs, wants
Something,
An interesting oddity
For this girl of color
Who stole the look, ways
And actions of movie stars
Playing their parts so well
They got their way.
"It works for them
And can for me."
All free for the taking
To grab, shape
And make it hers.
She was cute and funny.

But something got lost after
Years and added pounds
Too many days of sameness
Little knowledge of trends
Not staying current damaged
Cooled her appeal, and she
Didn't change, but kept using
Outmoded lines, sad moves
Obsolete, out of touch
Was caught in a time warp
Using what no longer worked.
Some of her antics got tolerated.
"She's not hurting 'nobody."
And she shared what she had
Food, information
Gossip and laughs.
She would strolled up to the
Day Shelter director:
"Can I come in the buildin' sir?
I need to go to the 'Baff-froom.'

"Mr. I need a bus pass," she said.
"I'm out!" he said.
"Gotta get back home," she said
Syrupy words draining out slow
Irritating, begging, running
Down coating her throat
Could drive you crazy
Count on her coming back
In the course of a day
As her needs increased
That's how she got tagged
And known as; "Big Baby!"
It was an everyday thing.
She's been answering
To that name every since,
"Hey! Big-Baby...!"
"Huh? What you want?
Hi! You got any cigarettes?
Where you been?"
Yeah, that's her. Big Baby!

COWBOY

Told I'm the strong silent type

One of a few blacks in the territory

You see or hear tell of that claims

To be a cowboy

Most around here act

Cool toward that kind 'a thing.

Don't want to be seen

Lookin and actin country

Lots of em stay as far removed

From down home things and

Thoughts as they can.

Ones here prefer

Sleeping on the street

Rather then being down home

Living on a place a' they own
Some raked together what they
Could and scuffled hard to leave.
Don't know why so many
Tryin' to erase a past where
They once was self-sufficient and
Raised most of what they ate, and
Could live, make do in a house
And on land that surrounded it.
At family reunions and gatherings
When everybody would come back
The house could fill up with folks
All there from near and far
Cities and towns all around
They sit, tell stories and tales
Glories of a nice new life that's *so*
Much better then in the country!
Up there it's heaven on earth!"
Curiosity, jealousy, and confusion
Abounds as to why they left

While we all stayed behind
Talk and lies swirl about as they eat
The fresh killed fried chicken.
The air fills with teasing, laughing,
As they chomp down on garden
Picked green beans and okra
There's talk, laughing while eating
"The best tomatoes I
Tasted in a long time!
Why y'all stay on down here?
Can do so much better
Up there!" they said.
"Need to come, stay, find a job,
'Git on your feet; get you a place.
Kids can go to better schools
Finish up, and college is free.
It'll be a whole lot better than
Eking out a living down here,
Think about it!" they said.
And most did just that

While digging in the yard
And weeding, watering the garden.
They thought while gathering eggs
And began to dread that life
It was on their minds when
They pulled on their dirty old
Work pants every morning.
They mulled it over and thought
About it when forced to get
Extra work in town just
To make ends meet.
It was clear when the wife
Had to go to work and help,
Soon they saw and knew that
It was the right thing to do.
They wanted nice things too.
Didn't they deserve better?
That life far away sounded good.
They wanted more than
Hard work and long hours,

What did they ever see in it anyway?

And so one day they just did it.

They packed, picked up, and

All headed off to the New World.

Hesitant, scared, but determined,

The family left to try and make their

Dreams come true in a place held

Up as the magnificent promise land

But soon things unraveled; unfolded.

Their urban hosts greeted them with

Weak smiles, surprised looks; and

The hope that it was a temporary visit,

Had there been a misunderstanding?

The only thing their new landlords

Could think was: "They bought it!

They believed all we said. "Maybe

It was a little *too* convincing.

Never thought they would do it!

What about the family reunions?

Where would they have them now?"

Down home they could spread out,

The children could run free.

There was room to have fun.

It was the perfect place to ship 'em

Off in the summers for two weeks."

They shook their heads in disbelief.

"They took us up on it!"

...down home? Me? Naw!

I didn't come from nowhere like that.

I'm from up around the northeast.

Fooled you, didn't I. This hat...?

Huh! Yeah, it's pretty big.

Biggest I could find.

If I'm gon be a cowboy,

I gon 'Be a COWBOY!'

But I'm more of a "wanna be."

A city slicker that come down

To pick up speech patterns

Most think they done got rid of.

That stuff hangs on like Bad breath!

Not even chewing two sticks
Of Gum can mask it.
I come here to study ways
Get hints from a past.
Like how to avoid eye contact.
Most times I stay to myself
But I watch and learn, preparing.
Got me a job I go to.
Then I come back here and
Sleep in the shelter at night.
'Preparing myself for that time
I move onto the land
And have my own place.
Yeah, they share with me,
Most not conscious they doing it,
I soak it all in. And I know
Won't be long till
I'll be moving on!

MARIO VEGA

Wants and needs to be who he is inside. He got a longing for the one he was born and cheated out of being. That image seemed just beyond his grasp. But time brought clarity. Years passed. Challenges helped strengthen and gave him courage to fight on. He had to and began accepting what was in his quiet soul all along. But he was scared, unsure having been too cautious at first to embrace it. He was told him over and over that he had a pretty face, and overheard some say he "should a' been a girl; you just too cute to be a boy!" He's still not sure he understood it right what they meant. But maybe he does. Or how else could he come to know that his outward form was plastic. He was smothering behind the mask. He might have passed out and even died if he had been forced to keep up the pretense too much longer. And then his moment came. It was the right time. He was feeling powerful enough to correct the charted path. He did what was needed to move on with all of who he was in tow. Now they call him a 'queen.' And he accepts the title. He was one of many who grew up in "The Big Apple," New York City, as Mario Vega, a black Puerto Rican. After that time he refused to continue that life he was imitating, and rushed out into his own world as Mario; and a few others labels, then Melissa. They all were him. But it wasn't easy. He had struggles. It was tough to break from that familiar pattern left for him. The way was out there, but it was hard to go and start true. But he did.

"Me and my husband decided we needed to be in that All-American City. ALL-AMERICAN! We wanted it to mean just what it said. And we wanted to believe it was a place the name implied, where all kinds are welcome. So we took off for our dream. Everybody we met when we got there was from someplace else. That "All-American City," the Utopia, called out to the world. But it was not long after that disappointment replaced excitement and naiveté. We tried to fake comfort and being hip. Maybe we were just not cool and savvy enough for most to fall for our hype. It was a game for suckers! Soon we were stuck and covered with hurts. Our disgust turned inward and toward each other, everything and everybody. Tempers flared and big troubles followed. I did jail time, and when I got back, my husband was with another queen. I wallowed in pity and hurt for a long time before I saw that it was not going to help. So I made a decision, 'pulled it in; made my way, got a place and started life anew. I didn't stay on the slab at night like some. Sometimes I got bored being away from real folks. And I'd go over to that gathering of lost souls and wanderers. I got along okay with the bums, but bosses in that place where we got handouts could be a pain. Inquiries, questions from inhabitants and more so from me could be met with surly answers and comments. "What did you say *Sir?*" Endless questions came from them and always ended with toying rudeness and that word, "*Sir.*" Their eyes would grow wide and confused. Quizzical looks shadowed contorted faces. That's when I always struck back. In my most outrageous tone, with attitude conjured up from legions of misunderstood drag queens throughout the ages; I'd hurl a tart response. "Si-r-r...?" I'd say, stretching the word beyond its limits. "Huh! You don't see 'no *man* standing here!" I said, admonishing him and anybody else around who was tempted to play *that* game. And then there was another time when the one in charge walked up to me making random conversation: "Mario, you *really* know how to fix your face and put on that makeup," he said. "Glad you noticed," I said, pleased by the compliment, but cautious enough to know it was an opening to more sinister thoughts soon to be revealed. I was told by too many to name that I was good looking, though maybe a bit overweight for now. Despite that, some said I looked more like a woman than others claiming to be. He kept talking like we were long lost friends catching up on some missed gossip. "Mario!" the director said. "Why don't you help Reg?" he said. Reg was another queen out on the street. "Help him how?" I said. "With everything!" he said. "He's got them full lips and the brightest reddest lipstick he can find smeared on 'em. And look at them big rusty feet hanging over some too little women's shoes. His hair's twisted in dreadlocks! Don't look like they seen water and shampoo in who knows when! And he got the ugliest makeup job anybody ever did see!" he said with a cackle. I looked at Reg and sighed. "Maybe some people just can't be helped!" I said. The boss nodded. "You do a good job with your makeup. Can't you do something for him?" he said. "Naw!" I said. "Some people are beyond even *my* help!"

We had some cold weather days and nights. And I went over to the center wearing pants and got asked about that. "You know," I was talking loud enough for everybody around who wanted to hear, and who might or might not be interested. "This cold weather almost made a *man* out a' me today!" I said. Days after that I was still wearing pants and the boss came up to me and said: "You still in pants! And you growing a beard too?" he said. There was the biggest surprised look on his face. "Yeah," I said. 'I'm wearing pants. That's right! So I thought I might as well grow a go-tee." I know they all wondered how long the change would last. Huh! I didn't even know myself. But it sure wasn' gon' change what was inside 'a me. That's what they don't understand. I was and always will be the same underneath the layers.

TIE MAN

Tie Man wears a suit coat and ten to
Twelve ties 'round his neck everyday.
You know it almost looks right.
And I guess for him it is,
Wouldn't recognize him without 'em
He's a alcoholic. Got a twin brother comes
Through every now and then checking to
See if he might a' become a loner.
He's the oldest. Memories of his
Mama's voice still haunts
And calls for him to watch
Out for his younger brother
He comes to the street searching
A shadow of worry covers him.

"Y'all seen my brother?" he yells and
Gets mad, nobody's paying attention,
Thinks he's talking to the deaf and
Crazy: "These folks got problems!
You all fools stayin' out here," he says.
"Lookin' for your brother? What's his
Name?" they say. "Harold," he said.
"Hair-ol...?" They repeat, mulling it over
"Harold!" He says it over and over again.
"Harold! Harol..." Then he remembers.
"Tie, Tie Man...!" He smiles, laughs
And is almost singing it out
"Oh-h...! Tie! Tie Man! Yeah!
Naw, I ain't seen him," they say.
"Damn man! Why didn't you
Just say so in the first place?"
They shrug, shake their heads as if
To say: "Hey, man! It's not my problem
He ain't been out here!"
Tie Man never talks. He goes here and

There picking up bottles, peering in

Poking around in trash cans.

He can never pass up a bottle

It calls out sending strange sounds

Gets his attention, catches his eye.

He'll sits at a distance staring at it

Folks wondering what he's doing:

"Why's he staring in that bottle?"

They learn what happened a while back.

That's when he lost one of his eyes.

Never wore a patch or treated it with

Medicine or nothing like he was told

One of them health workers helped

Took care, treated it for a while

But he didn't want help soon after

Didn't like folks getting too close

He said: being too close "cut his air."

He tried to do things on his own

But landed here on the concrete

And in the cold arms of the Slab

Somebody would get a couple of 40 ounces
The store would always gives as many
Free cups as you want.
They'd come back and pour up the brew
Pass it on and share it all. The one
Pouring always handed a cup to
Tie Man if he was around.
"Come on Tie Man! Here you go!"
That made him part of the group.
Was somebody that said he got
Hit right in that eye with a bottle
So now every time he sees one
He sneaks over to it real quiet
Trying not to disturb what's inside
And he'll get on his knees, bends over
Moves in close and when he's right
Up there on it he leans in.
They say he's looking for that eye he lost.
Could be... Maybe, just maybe he is.

SLAB WIFE

Concrete Woman of the street
Wants, needs the same love
Touch and feel as any other.
It's not a conventional home
With fresh warm sheets on a
Mattress atop box springs
No dresser or chifferobe
To store clothes with scents
Of odorous sachet bags that
Surround her personal items
No mirror to catch a glimpse
Of her body and face before and
After a night's pleasure and rest.

No door to close out

The world's existence

As they enjoy each other

Reliving days and years,

Airing dreams, tomorrows

No place to sit in comfort

Recline and stare up at the

Ceiling planning a budget

Or a fun evening out,

Living on the street her

Needs are magnified.

So many reasons

She came to be who she is

The main one is loneliness.

What's left is the false security

Of having a man, somebody to

Mull things over with till they don't matter.

Now she just wants to be with somebody

And that's about all she's got.

So it's all right for now, until

There's reason to want more.

Her needs are not the same

As his, another's or theirs

He wants the warmth

And source for his drive

The satisfaction of having

Someone to be with to

Show off and tempt others.

Insanity comes, there are no

Guarantees, rights, standards

Each takes the other as is

No questions asked, just more

Lies, hurts in shared moments

Of drug induced fake happiness.

Faithfulness is nonexistent.

Her man for the moment

And another's the next.

No loyalties or attachments.

No papers or life plan.

A nightmare in the face

And glare of day.
It's stupid, ridiculous
And inhumane
In all the created hours
As the days progress
Nothing is written down.
No contracts or blueprints.
Others without maps borrow
What seems a workable model
All are busy creating, cutting,
Fitting pieces they hope to
Use in their intolerable sham
Attached to this one now
And another the next
Earning a badge of dishonor
With no designated leader
Or model for validation.
Nothing is set in stone.
No judge or jury.
It's just the law of

The street that exists,
Application is seldom
Needed or wanted.
Hands off at this point
With both satisfied now
Until that shift comes
And so that's how it is.
Make the most of things
No apologies or
Excuses for herself
To or from anyone,
She'll stay, ride it out
Until it's over and done.
No expectation of anything
But whatever comes
She'll gather her courage
And grab hold.
Whether lessons sink in
Will only be known when
She's put to the test, and

Can summon what's needed
To live in hope for a better day

BAD WEATHER NIGHT

Bad weather alert!

The Day Resource Center

Becomes a night haven as

Street folks enter single file

In all states imaginable

Groups, couples, singles, sets

All there to take advantage

Of a rare great kindness and

Serious threat, weather alert of

Nighttime freezing snow and ice

Each enters and is counted

A total of one hundred

And twenty-three

Half are the regulars

That staff sees most days.

Others who heard about

The new policy show up

Some are familiar with the

Building and program; others

Enter scanning, looking,

Discovering new-found digs

Their palace for the evening

Not the usual space or dwelling

Their noisy nighttime presence

Sends a static charge through the air

Not a disruptive current,

But one of anticipation, relief

Excitement explodes all around.

The head man in charge decides

And wants to do something special

"Let's have a good night," he says
Then leaves, comes back later
Loaded down with treats for a
Party; there are movies they like.
"Not Christian stuff" they're told
That aims to minister the soul
And delve into their plight. No
It would not be so that night.
There was tasty food
And not a sorry faire,
It was a feast fit to serve
Heads of State,
A President would even
Be satisfied with such a spread.
Trays of every snack displayed
Fruits, cheese, and crackers,
Cookies, good fruits, sandwiches
Ice cream, and plenty of popcorn,
Candies, hot dogs and sodas
To feed and entertain the group

The next morning, a breakfast
Of donuts, coffee, juice, rolls,
For a happy settlement of souls
That good night, all had a ball.
It was a giant slumber-party
Where each room spilled over
And every hallway was full of
Thoughts adrift into a foggy past
Big talk, but no memory ever of
Such an invitation or gala
Some, a few had seen the like on TV
In movies; from bedtime stories read.
But that night with them all there
Ready for whatever was to come,
Lives and loads of stuff spilled forth
Robes, shower caps, house shoes
Things stuff in and pulled from bags
Slipped into, over, put on and
Paraded around to talk and visit.
It was a huge Celebration!

With small drops of happiness
So needed and long overdue
That was a good relaxing, easy time
A special night's run come true.

LIL' GARY

He's a short, thin little guy
Near him is one he calls son
There standing at his side.
It's his girlfriend's boy, but
He cares for him like his own.
Lil' Gary and his woman
Work everyday, come back
And talk about saving for
Their "dream house,"
Some place of their own to stay;
"Got a' find us a place!" That's what
They say almost everyday.
But at night they come back

And both smoke that 'crack
'Lil' Gary's got good intentions
He talks a good game
And you see that momma,
Diane, his girlfriend, sitting, waiting
For what she says is coming
A big lump sum of money that's
Due her, and is on the way from some
Unknown source she wouldn't say.
And it did come. But instead of doing
Right by her child, she and Lil' Gary
Took off to do something crazy; 'Crack.
Protective Services was called
To come pick up that boy
And it was then when
Something great happened that
Nobody could ever dream would be.
Street people got together, took over,
Cared and looked after that boy.
They did a super job of it too.

They watched out and kept him for
Four, five days like real parents do.
But even with all the good they did
Children Services came and took him.
And it wasn't no fault of there's.
What they did was true, right, and good.
He couldn't be left alone out there.
And when them folks took him, Ooh-wee!
Them was some mad bums
Out on the streets that day!
They cried and throwed stuff
Cussed that whole day and night
Into the next morning, and
Was still grumbling for a couple 'a
Evenings and days after that;
Nobody would 'a believed it
If they hadn't seen it
All that sadness and fire was coming
From some of the toughest, most
Hard-core street bums anywhere around.

They got mad and went out looking

For that mama and Lil' Gary; and

If they could 'a been found

They vowed and swore to beat

The hell "out a' both of 'em

Cause a how they did that boy and

Messed over that money they got.

Bums searched all down the "dusty trail"

Checked the road to the 'drug house'

At the end of the main path

But they didn't find them

Down there was all the same ones that

Always hung around buying, selling

Cocaine up and down that trail

The 'coke's the *dust;*

And the house where you get it

Sits at the end of the *trail*

CPS got that boy and sent him

On off to another town. They say

His mama's got three other kids.

The grand mama's got all of them now
That's the best thing for everybody
And they all know it too.
But for a few days that
Street family came together
And did good and right...

CHICKEN LADY / KISSIN' LADY

Didn't grow up straight-laced
And squeaky clean, neither
Did our elders, though most
From similar paths are wean
Church was our destination
Every Sunday morning
Saturday night bathed
Powdered and ready souls all sat
Present as the preacher's words extol
Repentance, goodness, and love for
Sinners scattered amongst the throes.
Bibles clutched tight in eager hands; try to
Shed worries of all that's left to do

Stopped agendas, projects, and plans
A vow to mind your own business
And keep the Lord's command.
Not an extraordinary bunch,
Just simple good folks
Would be our hunch, a
Lineage void of preachers,
Scholars, teachers and such
No missionaries, lawyers,
Bankers, politicians and
Others seeking our trust
We share quiet pleasures
Like Sunday evening rides
Packed tight together
In Daddy's black Buick;
Momma sitting at his side
And stops the regular places
Our hopeful wind-stroked faces set
Stern, in restrained anticipation
Peering out our rolled down window spaces

Collecting life and thoughts anew
Passing varied scenes we view
The ice cream parlor; grocery store
And at the journey's end, a place
Daddy never stopped before.
There we spy the crowds
Those setup hawking goods
Meant to quench and benefit
Needs from beginning to end
A swarm stands, hovers, talks
View a colorful array; and there
Reclaimed cigar boxes sit open
Curb-side to hold tokens from
A few with giving spirits who buy
As others stop, look, handle goods
Nod, talk, then strolls on by.
There's hope an interested heart or
Mind is touched by what they see
And will lean toward generosity
Could be a purchase will rid

Them of loathing and guilt
Bring hope, an offering of
Aid maybe even a better life.
Eight years later I met
Miss Dessie, the Chicken Lady.
I heard about her feeding the homeless
And that later it got to be too much.
Soon after she quit and left her work.
That had turned into a major
Feeding ministry; and helping enterprise.
Something about it gnawed at me.
Thoughts, pieces of visions and ideas
From that constant image, time and
Mission leaped and stayed in my mind,
I stopped resisting the call
Got in touch with her
She shared the vision
And I accepted the mission.
My confession of interest
Was the spark,

She applauded my desire
Pulled herself together
And was generous enough
To aid in reviving the dream
We worked up the plan and began.
In my search for purpose;
I found help and a friend.
Miss Dessie showed me
How to get donations
To prepare, serve, and
Where to find those in need
I worked, got myself ready to teach
And preach God's Word
Worked to give my best, to learn
Try to understand
Follow instructions
And so I started.
That was eight years ago today.
They call me a "Fundamentalist."
For some it means strict,

With an unwavering convictions
A Bible thumper who
Spouts platitudes and tidbits
A big part of the mission is
To greet everybody the same
With words of joy and excitement
"God Bless you! I love you!
Is said in Jesus' name"
All get hugs and kisses,
Anyone coming through the line
No one is ever by-passed or ignored
But rather welcomed and adored.
And with the help of volunteers
Dutiful, and alert
We continue the vision
Mission and work;
Ever seeking His guidance
And with purpose
To keep the faith as it was
From the beginning and still is

A team of hardworking
Dedicated women and men
Some of the same from that
Esteemed group remains today
Good, dependable, faithful
Sharing the love of God Supreme
No certain place is picked to serve
Nowhere is off limits.
Wherever they gathered
Is where it begins. On side-
Streets, the Day Resource Center
Or Dusty Trail; It doesn't matter.
It's about service without fail.
She drove a big pink
Lincoln Continental
You could see it for miles
Even far off up in the air
It got stole a few times
But the work and
Mission never stopped.

Sue L. Adkins

Things went on as usual.
The police found it on a vacant lot.

I'm treated like anybody else.
Sure, okay, I own things
I need, my possessions
But I'm no different than the rest.
Yes, I got my doubts, questions too.
Thugs and bums take advantage
They fight, lie, steal, and don't
Change just because they get fed.
We're all targets; them, me, and you.
Some street people are confused.
Whatever's convenient, they profess.
The Muslim faith one minute
And Christianity the next
They drink in front of anybody
Wherever they happen to be
Some think they got
The right to do dope and

Believe they need it to cope.

Others act like they ought

To be able to do anything

'Cause they're on the streets.

Yes. We still feed 'em.

Don't matter the story they give

Everybody gets treated like people

And with love and kindness

They are greeted all the same

"God bless you! We love you!

And it's said in Jesus' name.

DRIVE-BY FEEDINGS

They pull up here, over there, all around to bring breakfast and dinner without delay; the most important meals; the first and last of the day. Some come one or two days, often it's on a Wednesday or Thursday. But most are there on Saturdays and Sundays. The bounty is passed out or laid before the horde; with words, prayers and reminders that tell them it all comes from the Lord. Some are friendly, kind, though distant. "Their eyes and ways are cautious, "Handle with care," they seem to say. The hungry accept the goodwill choosing to ignore any looks of disdain. They take the faire and shower benefactors with joyous words of appreciation; "Thank you! Thank you!" It's their way of saying, 'we're glad you care.' Some who feed flinch and keep their distance. Still recipients are grateful they come. So many others stay away. 'Hey! We don't bite, you know!" Their words and faces say. Some show their gratitude with, "please and thank you;" heard in a steady flow that day.

These are scenes are reminders of Jesus in the Bible feeding crowds on the mountain. They come here too and bring their Bibles and preach. But not the loud yelping I remember back when I was young. Those memories come to me on occasion. My mama took us to town almost every Saturday morning. It seems like preachers stood on almost every street corner. A few claimed space at the busiest spots. They hurled stern words and quotes at crowds, and flipped through pages in the Bible, spitting out words with angry force. One preacher I remember was thin as a stream of smoke. His hair was shiny black, and done-up like Elvis. He always wore the same milk white Sunday dress shirt under a black thread-bare suit.

We got back home and mama was telling Aunt Mae all about him, laughing at how the shiny seat of his cheap pants was so slick; she said "him or whoever wore them before must a' done a lot of sitting and maybe even sleeping in 'em." She gave every last detail; describing each twist, sight and smell. I can still remember him with that tight high pitched voice. That got my attention and kept me listening. He would be set up right in the middle of the block, yelling and talking non-stop. He kept the words coming fast, then faster with a steady punch. You could never get all of what he was saying. The words shot out with such fiery and force; arms flinging, him spouting, blasting ears with whooping yells that nearly 'bout scared you half to death.

He'd point his long bony finger, then stopped, bend forward from his waist, and stick his narrow, scary face out, his bulging squinting eyes staring right straight into your soul and would shout loud as thunder, "J-e-sus!"

He was there most Saturday mornings in front of mama's favorite store. Behind him was a wide main street with passing cars, buses, delivery trucks, their brakes squealing. A few whizzed by on bikes dressed in delivery uniforms. Downtown was full of car sounds; motors sputtering; squealing brakes, and blaring horns. The traffic light changed and crowds rushed back and across wide streets moving, walking between that preacher and us toward their destinations; mothers with children straggling behind; and other shoppers who paid little attention to him or his words; some seemed annoyed. His keen-toed shoes fit snug hugging protruding bunions. Taps on the soles meant to stop run-over heels click-clacked with every shift, stop and stomp of his feet. He moved around, scratching groves in the pavement. Preparing to make a point, he leaned way back and sprang forward yelling scriptures rapid fire. He leafed through the book, never stopping to read, and spoke, reciting memorized verses to the temporary audience. Then raising and holding The Book up high, he spit out scriptures plain and pure. His ability would inspire some with words strong and sure. Never once did he consult a verse. But armed and full with the Word he spoke from last to first. He thumbed through that Book, not reading, and told truths to the wind and anybody who remained there to hear. His eyes held the hope they would take it and grow. His voice pushed forth in a quick staccato flow.

Most tried to avoid and not allow him to catch their eye. Could be it scared them to think he might delve inside; or that the words would force them to turn inward and peer deep into their souls. Most folks then were tough but polite. And his ways didn't seem to bother them. Some stood and listen; others did not, their minds elsewhere as they waited for the light to change. Then off they'd go. Some standing there rambling in purses for chewing gum, or piddling with their watch or chains. Brave ones and the foolish, kept their gaze fixed on him. He never faltered, not a bit. It was a sight to see because he didn't quit. He was selling nothing, just spreading the Word. I wonder where those preachers are now, if they are alive? Did the cities run them all out and away? Where did the go? Why didn't their sons and daughters step in and take their place? But that past is gone. At least I thought it was. It was years later that I happened upon that space. And there stood a preacher. Maybe it was the elder's son. He was dressed all in black. And it looked like he might be wearing his dad's same jacket and pants. This boy's wife stood close, her flowered print dress flowing in the wind.

And there was their son watching as his daddy spoke and mama sang to solemn stares. It was different. Not like back when I was little. The old time street preachers are gone now. The fire they had is stone cold. But the young ones still have something to say. They come and bring the Word and food. But there is little fire. We got so many new ones in the feeding game. They drive up, roll their window down quick, and hand the food out to you, and never get out of the car. They seem in a hurry the way they scramble to feed then drive off away and back to their nice warm homes. Some sit in cars talking on cell phones. Hey, don't get me wrong, I'm glad for them to come. Don't want it back like it was years ago. Yeah. Some of us can get food stamps now. But most of these hobos don't hold on to nothing and wind up right back here in line for daily feedings; them and me too. Not all of us want to be here though some do. Most don't want to tell their story how things happened. But for a lot of us it was quick and sure. Everybody's got a story. Today it's me and him. And tomorrow it could be you.

Yesterday life meant a house, family, a wife and kids. Then things come undone. See him over there? He worked hard and brought home his money. He was the man, the bread winner and king. But then it all fell apart. There was that time he found his wife with this other man. Things went crazy and he started screaming and yelling. "I'll kill him!" She was crying and begging. Then he just left, took off before he did something stupid. He was gone for weeks that turned to months. Once he got back to reclaim what was his, she was gone. He lost his job, friends, and everything else. Her family wouldn't say where she went. There he was left with nothing and nobody; all alone, without a friend. Soon there came a sad acceptance. He started begging, drinking, and drinking and begging. And he's still out here on the streets today; trying to find his way back to a place he can call his own.

SEX ON THE SLAB

It's out in the open

Viewed by all

For some a game

A challenge and ball

Who scores more points

Racks up the numbers

Finds and conquers

Scores of victims

Who's got the gall

Gets the most notches

Leaves strings of bodies

Influenced by sixties and seventies

Cries of free love with no guaranties

Voyeurism permitted, tolerated
Accepted as the norm
Mental score cards kept
On who did what to whom
In so many different ways
Ugliness so prominent
Accepted by some
Ignored by others
As vile and dumb
Ranked by like needs
A preference made with
Little and no attention to
Health, safety or creed
An attitude of this society
The nineties amplified.
It can all happen in
Out of control, haphazard
Inadequate, poorly monitored
Areas in the organized
Chaos of the streets

One of a few places
They're left to congregate
Where citizens accept
Bazaar behavior
And seem Resigned
Ready and willing to tolerate
Encourage, show and train
New ones who arrive
The contagious have no
Qualms about exploiting others
And some participants
Are willing to risk it all
Health and life
As though there's a mandate.
Most seem not to care.
They want what they want.
The rest of the world is soon
Viewed as foes and irritants
"Nobody gives a damn 'bout me!
Huh! I'm gon' die with something...!"

There's a don't care, blasé attitude
And demeanor, reaction to
Their plight spreads like wildfire
There's sex out in the open
On the streets in full view
To anybody who passes by
Some stand around
Cheering, urging them on
Smiles, laughs, and hoots of glee
Advantage taken of the vulnerable
Young men, women and children
And all of its done with total
Disregard for humanity.
This life's not meant for humans.
So many are reduced to
Base and savage instincts
It's survival of the fiercest.
The road back is long and bleak
Once the line of humanity is crossed
Most never make it out and back

And some others refuse to try.

Those not content to live that life

Learn to steer around, through the strife.

Novice to the slab must be separated

From them and lead back to civility

Vultures try to grab and hold on

Tight for as long as they can

But even those lives in peril

Can be saved and made stronger.

The hard-core are out to corrupt

And add as many as they can

To their miserable ranks

And to build a following

Every measure is tried. With

Enticements, lies and drugs

Using the guise of helpful friend

And all the leaches are bent

On sucking as much decency out

Of as many, every victim as they can.

Homeless for Now

Can this be my home?
The place where I live?
Yes, for now it is.
How did it start?
And where will I end?
Mama had big plans for me
College, marriage, kids
A house and car for sure
I was her lucky start.
She had her "boy!"
A good delivery
No problems.
She was strict.

"Don't be bad," she said.
"Stay 'way from them streets!
Don't be like your daddy!
Hey! Uh-uh! Stop that!"
She chided.

"Put that down!
I told you not to do that!
Now I'm gon' whup your butt!"
"Naw mama! Naw!
I didn' do nothin'!
I didn' do it!
I ain' gon' do it no mor'
Mama! Aw, mama!
Oh-h! Naw!"
"Didn't I tell you...!
You gon' mind me!"
"Yes 'ma'am'!"
He cried; then sulked.
Dreamed up cruel revenge

"Come here!" she said
He saw tears in her eyes
"Baby, now you know
I don't want to whup you
But I ain't gon' have no lyin'
She said.
"Yeah 'ma'am," he said.

I know you see
Where I am now Mama,
But I didn't mean for it
To turn out this way
I know it was hard
And you had to do it all.
After a while you couldn't
Help. You stopped trying
It was so hard
And you got tired
Working two jobs
Coming home

With nobody to help plan
And share your dreams.
There was that
Occasional body
But no real attachment
To you and none to me
No concerns for your needs
You wanted a man to hug
And give tenderness and love
To share your burdens
Joys and smiles
But you just had
The problems
And a hard-headed
Stubborn boy
I'm sorry mama!
So sorry!
What can I do?
Where do I go?
I don't know

There's nobody I can call on to

Get to listen to who understands

What I need, and there's

Nobody I can get through to

Who'll be there and help me

Figure out what to do

Nobody to push and point me

In the right direction

There are so many roads

And people all around

But few have my interest at heart

Some are spiteful and full of envy

I need help and time to identify

So I'll know the difference.

I'm back out now, and free.

Without shackles, bonds

And still there's nobody to

Help me with self-control

Advice on how to proceed

What direction to go, the

Correct responses to make.
I can't remain the old me
Who am I now?
Am I the old me, the new, or
Am I somebody in between?
I had to leave it all behind
And start fresh.
Now I go where I want.
Eat and sleep where
And when I choose
And talk when I decide.
Life turned me loose.
Sure, I'm Homeless for now.
But I'm on my way back
I'll get it right this time.
You'll see.

LIES...

Why all the lies?
So many told when you
Need to make a change
To stop and be bold
Nothing means a thing
Nobody cares about me.
How and when it happened
Is hard to remember
Faked being cool and in control
Till I was forced to face time
And make my own moves.
It was hard to wait
To be told what to do

When to come and go
On my own I learned
To accept yes and no
A big boy or a fool
But soon I found
I could make it
And needed no one
Like all the others
Wandering 'round out there
I was resigned to accept my lot
Fate and fears
I do the best I can
Even though many
Want much more for me
To do good now
I decide to work hard
Toward my own destiny
I want things and
People in my life
Real people, true-blue

But I stayed too long now

The way is gloomy and foggy

It would take a master guide

To chart and help steer

My travel through endless

Darkness into the light

There are reasons and

Things can seem impossible

Others see worthlessness

And seldom look at me

Or acknowledge my existence

I still believe I can do and be

I watch them drive up

In homes on wheels

Not once do they see who I am

Or care about hurts I feel

I'm just a blur, a statue, a stone

They throw a bit of grain my way

Then leave and I'm alone.

I hate them.

I hate me, my life.

I hate it all!

Do I drink?

Yeah. I do.

It soothes me

Makes me feel young, tall

Popular, desirable

And whole

My kind of folks out there

They take me like I am

If I got money everything's good

When I don't, I'm po'r Sam

Can sit for hours, pass the bottle

Talk and lie about ourselves

We laugh, joke and seldom worry

About anything that matters

Between us and them

In that outside world

We got the answers

And convince ourselves

With idle chatter
One day I'll get it together
Find a job, a house
And a good women
Family and children will
Come one day
Mama will be proud
I'll do it up right!
I know I can
The way she planned for me
One day soon it'll happen.

OUTSIDER

It's tiring and sad seeing

All the mess, waste

And fading lives abound

As we labor in this work.

Most don't seem to get it or

Know what they need to do.

While some are not serious

Others feel hopeless and know

That it's not right for them.

No. A good life's not promised.

Many act like it's a run-through.

But this is it! Only one per customer

Some work, improve; try to do right

Believe and treat it precious and dear.

But for those who don't, I say listen!

He ain' fooling people!

(Points to the Bible)

I carry this book daily,

And clutch it tight.

There's a need to share

His Words and I pray with

Heart-felt abundant might.

I've seen it time and again.

They come to feed, see and hear.

We explain as a fragile flock complains.

We emphasize and even baptize.

We hug, kiss and cry; there are

Some we miss, but still we hope

And pray the Word gets to most.

A few listen and hear. Once it's given

Then we talk, sing, pray, feed again

And continue to share and try

To help them see. Things can

Seem hopeless at times even to us.

They sit, some not listening, unaware,

Laughing, talking as we explain.

Some others ignore us, yelling

Greetings to passersby; our

Attempts to reach hearts and minds

Through the lesson is met with sighs.

"We can stay stagnate for just so long.

After that we dry up, rot, and die!"

We pray, hope to get their attention

And make them see it's for all eternity.

The work and God's message goes on.

We pray, sing, urge with tons of love.

And look to the One who is The Way.

What do you do to reach the lost?

Go where they congregate,

Take them the powerful message

And pray that it will be applied.

Zany craziness goes on, continues

But people still need help. They do.

It's trying. Work out here can be a zoo.

Freaks, crazies, those depressed, the

Throwaways let it all hang out. You

Try to get and hold their attention.

Remain steadfast, explain that the

Street life is counterfeit, can't last.

The gathered lost souls you try to turn

Around, move past the dead ends; but

There on the streets dwell walking corps

Tortured souls their carcass soon shed.

Most are drained of courage, can't face life.

Pus builds, festers and grows, becomes

A draining scourge; out of ignorance,

Disgust, condemnation, passiveness, we help

Perpetuate, justify, and later try to control,

Market and then take charge and fix. Soon

We can't handle, remove or stop it. You

Watch it grow, some expire, but more come

And while it lives, continues and breathes,

A system develops that feeds on need

Builds up around it spreading
The wound, stench and decay
We may never get them all
To know, understand, to
Move on, and make a good life.
But there can be successes
Though they may seem small
Invisible, not worth the effort
Except to the Heavenly One
That we call upon. But every
Success is a help to us all.
We yearn to clean things up
Make them neat and tidy.
But only He knows how we can
Rid ourselves of the ugly waste.
And with His help, Yes
Through Him the Almighty
Are things done.

THE DRINKING TREE

(A Call For Cities To Take A Stand)

"Remember that time?" He begins.
A light clicks on for one of the
Many human throwaways
There in the crowd.
"Yeah, that's Right!" Words of
Affirmations push forward.
A few stare with intent
Wanting to lean and hear more
From this self-anointed Griot.
He continues: "We slept over on..."
He stops and reflects to crystallize
Thoughts, memories, and

The experiences that go with
Some image in his head.
"Un-huh yeah, that's right!
Come on wid it now!"
His audience coaxes, urges him on.
"It was a real trip!" he say.
Floods of "Amen's" spilled from that
Temporary group of worshippers
"Yeah you ain' lyin' man!" they said.
He waits on his thoughts.
"I never moved, ran from, or lived
In so many places in all my life
I picked up from here to go there.
Was never one to stay too long
Now that's freedom.
Our people know 'bout that!"
He turns up the bottle and
Takes a matter-of-fact gulp
"We still go through the same stuff"
He assured the unholy congregation

Strewn around the drinking tree
It's their regular meeting place.
A shady clubhouse without walls
Where everybody is welcome to
Come, sit, hear and tell stories
Their own versions of truth and lies
All the news and gossip of the day and
Events of the night are delivered at
The sad mimic of a bar and social club
Where trouble is common, a game
Smokes and forty ounces mellow the
Crowd, aids the telling of tall tales
And remembrance of dim yesterdays
Each one adds on made up parts
And fashions it to suit the moment
It's all a big lie and they know it.
But that's one way to be included
And become part of the group
History pulled from faulty memories
Merge with spin and hallucinogens

In arguments and fights
But most of its fun, good times
They come with music, tunes
Blaring from their past
And create a stage
To sing and dance
Lit cigarettes dangle from taunt lips.
All are urged to join in.
Soon everybody's involved.
Finding their circle and groove
For a brief time most everybody
Gets caught up in the revelry
That lasts till reality steps in.
Awkward merriment, riotous behavior
Marks and label a scene abnormal. Some
Things that happen in the open air
Of the streets should not, and
Must not be accepted or tolerated.
Those things are meant for the privacy
Of home or maybe in a nightclub

You see folks in hair rollers

In robes and house shoes

Visiting, mingling, lounging

Like it's a natural thing

But it's not.

Personal needs should not

Be attended to in public view

On downtown and public city streets

And we cannot make it

Anything other than what it is.

Unacceptable!

This is public space

Not a private boudoir

And it cannot be allowed

Ignored or treated as normal!

Public streets should not be seized

And claimed as personal space

Or used as a camp.

You are to relax at home.

We cannot, should not ignore

Or sanction lax activities
Of people living on the streets
As though it's their home
It's improper and should
Be made unacceptable.
It cannot be tolerated.
It must be seen as abnormal
And shameful
We can't continue to excuse
Unacceptable behavior
Because of a present condition
We must not overlook and ignore this
Or let human dignity erode and disappear.

RAILROAD WORKER

He earned good money
And was a hard worker
Told he was one of the best
But a horrid scourge took hold
MADNESS came and hovered
To descend and bore down
Deep, embedding itself within
And soon he came to know
Desire, need and Love it
What he did was 'Crack.
And he had to have it.
Before that he made money
Working for the railroad
And spent it all on the charmer

His woman stayed silent, joined in
Accepted, approved, tolerated it
Stuff that had him broke, sick
She used and needed it too.
They cultivated their weakness
A mutual habit, as proof of love
Wake-up came fast, hard; the signs
Ahead read Destruction! Death! was
A clue to stop, turn his life around
Get quiet, relax the mind and think
Why do some give in, latch on and
Go through so much bad stuff?
Warnings come, signal trouble ahead
Evil lurks, excites; makes it seem fun
Clues, warnings come and tell you to
Turn, move, run, don't be consumed
You see it's bad, there's a need to pray
To ask for wisdom and guts
All the stories you tell amuse
And draw in other losers, with

Attention focused on you and them
And the more horrendous a scene,
The greater the interest and spotlight
Will shine on the bums and hustlers

His name was Ben.
He worked steady for a time
For maybe ten years or more
His life was under control
Until it, that thing seemed
To get the best of Him
He took on more and more jobs.
That became his life and world.
But things started slipping
Not going right, and got messed up.
He talked to "the man," told him he'd
Work harder, try to get it together.
But his boss saw sickness in his face
"Nah... take some time off.
"We'll pay for treatment," he said.

"I'm gon quit!" was Ben's retort.
He was sure he could find
Work later when he was ready.
"Hey! I don't need this!
I'm good at what I do!" he said
Yeah. Sure. A lot he knew.
The money, a place to live,
And his ole lady all left.
Now on a destructive path
Headed for the place of no return
Things got hard; it was an eternity
His regrets piled high. But he
Stopped long enough to hear
Other sad stories of what it took
How to conquer and maintain
He'd always made money
The right decent way
But things got twisted, strange
He talked others into his craziness

It was wrong to fool with the

Demon, and doubly so to

Get others to do the same.

But that wasn't his worry.

Money and taking care

Was all he had on his mind

That, plus selling, scoring...

He made and got the bills

And turned it all into crack

Now everything was about him.

Life was turning and smoking.

Here's his story:

"That day I cashed my check

Got my stuff

Found the right spot

Settled in to light my pipe

And that's when I saw this

Evil smiling ghoul-man in the mist

I looked through half-shut eyes.

But it was hard to make out who
That intruder was in my shadow
And I never once lowered the pipe
Not even for a second.
I strained, peering, hoping
I wouldn't see who it really was.
But I knew... it was the devil!
There standing in my shadow.
And all around was hazy-gloom
It had this cold, froze up leer.
Then that devil inched up to me
Came so close we got nose to nose
And that's when I saw it was... *Me*!
I kept staring at my reflection
But it looked different now
It was my body turned inside out
And was covered in mucus and worms
I saw that my eyes and mouth
Had a death grin fixed across it, strong
That's when I throwed down that pipe

And went to screaming and yelling

Oh! I was shaking so in terror

That I took off running, trying

To get away from that sight

Every night after that

When I lay down to sleep

That horrible vision came.

Hell chased, was catching up

And trying to take a-hold a' me.

It went on and got more unbearable.

Sleep wouldn't come; wasn't knowed

I had to purge the intruder out, away

If I was to have any kind of peace

That strange and hard time was

A never-ending nightmare

With few options

That's when I stumbled

Was lead or seemed to

Roll into the sanctum of

A church mission

I didn't want to be there
And tried to turn around
Like I had done before
Always thought I could
Do fine on my own.
But it seemed now I couldn't
Not how I was now, like this.
What got me to this place?
Was it pride, arrogance? And
Now fear in a self-absorbed Life?
I wanted to step back to yesterday.
I had been comfortable there.
The fear was slow to fade. And then
What looked to be Saints, appeared
Their outstretched arms cradled me
Gave care with offerings of more
And the assurance that things
Could be different, good, and
Life could be real, livable again.
My feet froze solid, I stayed put

Couldn't turn and go back.
Now I could only move
Forward into goodness that
Was once so unfamiliar
But my fear paralyzed me.
My mind knew I didn't want the
Strange forbidding thing ahead
My body was hard like cement
And was froze and in pain
Like a trapped trembling prey
Now facing a territory of love
I accepted without further delay
Thankful I was no longer
Be held by that vile scourge
As I relaxed, a warm midst
Covered me, saturated and brought
A crystal clarity that said
'This is your beginning'
It has been two years
And none of it's been easy

The trail to sanity is rocky
With many remedial steps
But rebirth can occur.
When it does,
Time will open and
Force every nerve, vein
Muscle and cell to restart
So what you must do is
Make the necessary effort
Believe you are worthy.
No. It's not easy
But it is possible.
Welcome it with
Body, soul and spirit,
It's the way to expel evil
And reclaim the veiled
Good, worthwhile and purposeful.

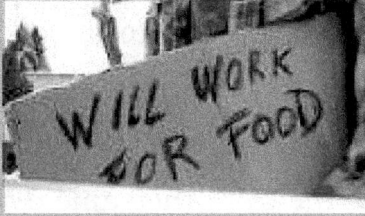

Offers of food and coupons

For fast food places nearby

A feeble invitation to dine after

The pitch and plea for help

Can result in vile looks and words

Staked claims to lucrative corners

On Downtown city streets are

Unwelcome sites where

They stand alone, dressed

In desperate garb to get

Attention, touch minds

And hearts of all kinds with
Persuasive hope passersby will
Give a sum of money that exceeds
Or is equivalent to the effort.
Some with kids, unwashed, grimy
Hopeless and distant seeming to have
All emerge from the same dirt pile
Faces, clothes smudged with grease
Grim, stern looks of desperation
And neglect to body and spirit
"We not hurtin' nobody!" they say.
Maybe... It could be. But
What about dignity and pride?
Some are better at the work
"Huh! You can make more here
Than on some job," they say.
Generous ones don't judge
They share and help, give
What's done with it is between
The receiver and their Maker

Others disgusted, ignore
Stare panhandlers down
With mean glares, warning
All to stay far away
Most have stories, a few
Come early to stake claim
On special turf and places
Some veterans in uniform
And others non-military
Stand and make their plea
A few sit in wheelchairs, others
Pace or sit and wave, holding
Hand-painted cardboard signs
With familiar requests for help
Right over there is Milton
An admitted alcoholic
He drove a truck for years
Got married for a time
But let his temper and
Unfaithful ways ended it.

Years later when he couldn't
Get his life on track, he made
Contact with his ex for help. She
Did what she felt was her duty
Took him in, got him going to AA
Paid for training to increase his
Knowledge; he got a trade and
Was ready for a decent paying job
But he kept his roving ways.
Once training was done he
Rejected every offer that came
Everything that was offered him
She'd had enough, kicked him
Out and sent him on his way.
Driving to her job one day she
Stopped at a light about
Five feet from some homeless
Figure, standing, holding a sign
Was nothing unusual about it
Somebody stood there everyday

Like part of the landscape, but
Something about this one was odd.
She didn't know why but she
Sat staring at him for a long time.
He had a strange and familiar pose.
Something about it gnawed at her
Why was she focusing on him?
She shook off silly thoughts
That crept into her head.
But more pressing things,
Issues crowed her mind.
She felt good that she could
Look at him with compassion.
Something about it sort of
Shook and kept her attention
She sat watching him until
The light turned green, then
She drove pass, on her way.
Something made her turn around
And go back to that intersection.

Crazy thoughts popped in her head
She had visions of her past, tons
Of memories rushed in her mind
And that's when she realized
She knew him. It was "Milton!"
Her rational self didn't believe it,
But her thoughts and curiosity
Made her turn the car around
And speed back to that corner.
Her heart was racing. Somehow
She knew it was no mistake.
It didn't take her long to get
Back and park. She sat there
Watching as he stood in place.
Was it him, or was she mistaken?
She had to know for sure.
She didn't want to run into him
Another time and start joking,
Accusing him of being *that beggar*
She saw on the corner, and

Have him give a convincing denial.

No. Not unless she had proof

And she was sure.

She got out of her car

And walk over to him.

His look of destitution and

Slumped body was poised

Position for his audience to

Behold a dispossessed, unloved one.

She was never one to back down

When confronted with a dilemma,

This would keep her record in tact.

"Milton?" she said. "Milton!"

He jumped, startled, remembering

His mother's call upon discovering

Trash still sitting in the same spot

Where she left it that morning

Her instructions had been ignored

He'd gone outside instead to play

And shoot marbles with his friends.

He made a slight turn toward her and
Kept himself positioned not wanting to
Take a chance on missing a donation.
She called his name again with
No concern for his days' receipts.
"Milton! What are you doing?"
His face showed no hint of shame or
Apology, "Oh, hey Ruth, baby."
He spoke like he'd just got home and
Was greeting her after a day at the office
"Milton what the hell's goin' on with you?
What is this all about?
You done lost your dang mind!
Oh, hey! Hey baby, naw!
Ain't nothing like that!
I'm just doing what I do!
This is my thang! I *do* this!
I'm good at it too," he said.
"Milton! Why you out here?
You ain't no dummy!

You been to school, and
You can get a job!" she said.
"Doing what?
Driving a damn truck?
Done that! Anyway, nobody's
Paying entry level men
Good money these days!
Baby I'm too old to start fresh.
But this here I can do.
It don't take training
And I can work my own
Hours," he said with a smile.
If I don't feel like going in
It ain't no-body's business.
I don't have no 'straw boss
...ain't got to play no games.
I can handle this
And I'm doing fine at it.
I take in enough for rent and to
Buy my food and dope," he said.

"Milton, you must be crazy!
You came to me not long ago
And I took your sorry butt in!
I let you stay with me free!
Fed you, got you in training
So you could get a decent job
Not to stand out on a corner, a
Begging bum! I can't believe it!
You must a' lost your mind!
That dope's done wiped it out!"
She said. "Hey! Listen! Ruth!"
"You did all you could
To help and I appreciate it.
You' been good to me
But I got to do things my way!
And this is how I'm gon' do it
No matter what nobody else
Thinks about it, this is 'my way!'
I ain't hurtin nobody," he said.
"I know," she said.

"...nobody but yourself.

This ain't no way to live!

You can do better.

This is for people at the

End of their rope. You don't

Have to do this!" she said.

"I do. I am. Now that's it!

That's how I want it," he said.

There was a long pause.

She stared at this stranger,

He looked away, wanting

To get back to his business;

"I'm doing what I want.

I'm fine," he said.

He talked on, explaining.

Maybe he was just confused and

If she could keep talking, trying to

Reason with him, maybe

It would bring memories and

Trigger something that would

Snap him back to reality.

"Milton? Why?

I don't understand," she said.

"Don't try," he said.

"I'm gon' do this.

It's what I want.

You don't have to

Take care of me no more.

I can do for myself.

Go on now," he said.

His words came

Out clear and easy,

Sweeping through her mind,

Changing a raging storm to a

Calm sunny day.

"You headed to work?" he said,

Smiling, talking as if they were

Home and she was waking him

From a dream; "Yeah," she said.

She got caught up in his fantasy.

He had that effect on her.

Still she didn't understand.

He wasn't handsome.

What did she see in him?

It was hard to explain.

She knew she loved him

And would take him back if

He would agree to come.

She gestured away in

No certain direction.

"Gotta' go to work," she said.

"Yeah, all right," he said. "Go,

And let me get back to mine.

I'll call if I need help," he said.

"Milton, I just don't know.

It don't make sense," she said.

"Maybe not to you, he said.

It's only got to make sense to me."

He paused and looked away.

"See you around," he said

And that was it.
There was no further discussion.
She waved goodbye, turned her
Attention to the oncoming traffic
And when it was clear she dashed back
Across the street to her car; got in,
Started it up, sat there awhile and
Looked over at him standing
Back in the place she found him.
He seemed all right but
Had that blank stare of
Desperation stuck on his face.
She watched a car pull up to him.
The window came down and
A hand jutted out holding a dollar bill.
Milton went over and grabbed his pay.
He nodded a thank you and walked
Back over to his post.
It seemed natural for him.
But it sent chills over her.

She calmed herself down and
Realized it was Milton's choice.
That was how he wanted things.
And there was nothing she could do
Or say to change it.
He was grown, free to make his
Decisions; and that was that.
If that's what he wanted,
Then so be it!
He wasn't her child.
She sighed, pulled onto the street,
Made a U-turn and drove on by.
He never looked in her direction.
All she could think was:
'May God bless him
And all the others like him.
She had done all she could.
Now he was in the hands
Of a Higher Power

THE DUSTY TRAIL

David went through

Good and bad days

For thirty-two years

He felt frail and empty.

His was an East Texas heritage

Made up of Teachers, Doctors

And a couple of Lawyers

College meant he'd carry on that

Collection of pursuits and goals

Discussed, passed on, embedded

Deep down in his mind and soul

But it brought challenges and a real

Disconnect with his family and past

It clogged his mind so he swore

Never to return home again

Soon fear that his vile reputation

Would bring shame and scorn

On the ones he looked up to

Respected and once held dear.

He got hooked on drugs.

Nothing could stop him from using.

In his head things were going well.

He had no problems in his books.

Never a hint he might fail.

Everybody there did a little

Something to help cope

Marijuana was preferred.

Called the mighty "vine of hope"

It seemed an unusual comparison.

He was nudged to tag along

And go party, though he was

Cautious and held back some.

He paced himself, studied, the

Thoughts stayed in his head how

His folks paved the way for him.

He had to keep up his work
And do well in all his classes.
No time for left for partying
But maybe they'd understand
If he took some time off to relax
And enjoy things a little.
He monitored himself and did
Well the first year and second.
The third was much harder.
His courses got tougher and
The women more demanding.
He tried to juggle things
And fit it all in.
Still he hung out some
Played a little ball
And got pretty good until
Soon he was the all around guy
The one everybody was sure
Would be the one to make it
He just needed to stay

Strong and keep going.
Some of the best, toughest, brightest
Stumbled and fell, never to rise again.

Late nights and hanging out
Didn't leave much time for
Academics after a while
Something had to give.
Pills came from here and there
A way to ease the way, calm nerves
Rejected at first with looks of dismay
He did good at first, was bold, refused
But he accepted after a while.
Then it got easier until
He got to be a steady participant.
Soon he was the "one"
They should see for a little relief.
He didn't much like his new appeal
But it was hard to push it away.
His habit got so bad

Life as usual was not an option.

He was hooked.

His family was disappointed

But anxious to help him

Get back to how he once was.

"Re-hab" was the first step.

But once he got out, old

Habits burst forth with fury.

His family backed away in disgust

And told him they would

Be there to help when he got

Ready to tackle the problem,

For now he could count them out.

And until that time came

He would bear his shame alone.

He was part of the group on the streets

That made the trek to the "Dusty Trail"

That way-station for users

Dopers and crack smokers.

Now he was one of the regulars.

Some go there with money to buy
Others take stolen merchandise
Their possessions to trade
And make some kind of deal.
They do whatever is needed
So they can get "the dust."
The Trail leads right to where
You got cocaine and crack.
Everybody knows about it
That includes the cops
And others at City Hall
It gets to you knowing
How it's used to control.
Regulars are known by name.

David got in a fight down there.
I'm told he was high, got 'jacked
And he beat the hell out of
Some guy and killed him!
He got five years in the pen

And was never the same again
He did hard time; when they let
Him out he wasn't no good
To nobody, soon falling back
Into his old ways heading off
Down the Dusty Trail; and then
He stopped, got his head cleared
And was back on target again
Until things got to be too much
Those times would just
Fill him up with fear.
Thoughts triggered things
That got him using again
And made him want to end it;
His attempts to erase memories
Of the pain kept throwing him back
Then something would grab hold
Pull him out, and he got help that
Lasted awhile,; nothing lasted
One day he stumbled into my office

As Director of the Homeless Center
I knew about his history and saw
That perplexed look on his face
"David what you gon do?
You're no dummy; you got brains
At least for the time being,
Better use 'em man!" I told him.
"Find a job; get back on your feet
People here can help you.
You got to get it together
And stop the drugs man!
He sat staring with a blank look.
"Man-n, ain't no help for me!
"None!" he said.
And he told me his nightmare.
"Know what I feel like doing?"
His face was cold. He had a blank stare.
"I feel like taking a big brown paper
Grocery bag, filling it up with coke
Sticking my head in

And sucking up every last bit!
Then he leaned over forward
Bent at the waist; head jutted out,
His balled up fists pressing
Into either side of his face,
As if to hold his ears in place
Waiting, until the glue dries
He had a wild maddening look.
"I would snort every bit up and
Wouldn't take my head out
Not till it was all gone!" He said.
I'd keep my head in until I died.
Yeah! That's what I want to do.
And it's all I dream about doing.
That's my every thought," he said.
After he was done telling his tale
His face got strange, twisted; scary.
That's when I gathered every ounce of
Force I could summon and spoke up.
It wasn't loud. But I said it with

Power and strong feelings of disgust

Words pushing against my clenched teeth;

Get up! Get the hell outta' my office! Now!

I don't want *no dead* folks in here!

People out here to help, encourage,

Trying to get you to do right!

You got the nerve to sit here in *my*

Office and say crap like that?

Get UP! Get the hell out!

And don't come back

Until you're ready to live!

He didn't say another word.

I was his misplaced conscience

That was lost a long time ago.

He jumped up, turned

Rushed, and bounded on out the door

And that was just fine with me.

No dead defeated folks allowed!

That was the sign I needed on my wall

For all those determined to be losers.

It was hard enough working, trying
To help the ones who wanted to live
And were trying to do better
But it's darn near impossible with those
That's got some crazy death wish.
"I don't want to hear it!"
I yelled out after him as he left.
"Go off and do it someplace else!
This is not gona' be your grave!
Not while I'm here!" I haven't
Seen or heard from him since.
He's can't forgive himself and
He's not willing to be forgiven.
He won't let you help him
And he's forgot about God
That's why it's so important for
The churches to keep coming,
Bringing food; offering hope.
There's always a chance
Somebody will be helped and

Can forgive and accept forgiveness.

David needs to hear that message.

He has a lot to give and he can have

A life if he allows himself that option.

But he's got to stop wallowing in the past.

Even his horrific sorrows can be forgiven.

And maybe he can help somebody else.

He's got to forgive himself in order to live.

B.U.B.S

Bums Under Bridges

Freeways trail through manufactured
Hills and ebbs an expanse of sky
Climbing mounds of grassy fields
Forming the artificial boundary
Between a mesh of earth and lives
Know that semblance of protection

Cannot shield bitter tears
Merciless weather, terror and fears
Housed in various forms of containment
Forced out, shooed to journey, adrift
Carrying lives packed in old satchels
Wrapped in newspapers, blankets, quilts
Stored up memories time eliminates
Minds that stall, fail to recall, refuse to
Pass on, disseminate; so reviled, not
Wanted, unwelcomed, the accused
Others resented, some demented
Many confused and viewed
Daily by folks not amused.
Most take the abuse, looks of
Disgust, accusation and blame
As eyes meet with caution, hatred
Wonder and shame. Pallets, plastics,
Trash, all re-shares the landscape.
Bed-rolls and grocery carts full of stuff

Tied down, spread out, overflowing

Covers space and place so bold

Is scattered about in exact chaos

Can make it look dank and cold

A mix of nature's fragrant bounty

Blooms full a sad array unfolds.

Human refuge is what's planted

No concern for its fit in the display.

Wide and narrow shadows emanate.

Tall buildings pike, spike all around.

Standing straight, sharp, bold, piercing

A sky hot and bright; so little shade

A want is found everywhere around.

Beauty and ugly share the space

With intolerance, lacking patience

And not a smattering of grace

Makeshift spaces, stuffed bundles

Tied together with rope and shoelaces

No furnished place, quite the contrary.

An old mattress plopped down; a bed

For two who seek rest at the end of day

Some exhibit a tough exterior; facades

Of protection; false measures of cheer

Eerie, alone, clever phantom beings

Any semblance of humanity long forgotten

Urban squatters settle land to which

They bear no legal ownership or claim

And get lulled into degrading changes

That reduces them to base beings

Nudged and soothed into false freedom.

Participants in shameful, violent deeds

Contemptuous, boisterous, vile acts

Degrading words spewed at strangers.

Lends sad worth to images, patterns,

Circumstances, challenges that trap

Many who come to see it as normal

Others look on with pity, shame

Those pious and plain see a show

And believe it to be the model. But

Never go deeper to uncover the truth.

Official attempts to hush the most vocal
Those visible, obvious ones who offend
Quiet the clatter, allowing preachers
And teacher to come and minister
To love, feed and show they matter.
Will create and keep a fake peace for
As long as it takes those who need it,
And give some time to recover
For them and society's sake
It's so easy to say, but hard to do when
Authority looks on from far off. But
Sympathy and attempts don't fix things.
They only slow and temper eruptions
It manages to quiet the noise awhile
As the tide rolls out and takes it
Away and removes some disruptions.
Bosses try to put out fires, stem impulses
Allow gatherings with coffee, fried potatoes
And once the fun time is done comes a sigh

As most sit back, laugh and tell lies.
Then you watch them dance
While a few cry, pray and hope things
Get better before they die.

~End~

Sue L. Adkins

Sue L. Adkins is a poet, novelist, an author of Children's books with music, a playwright, actress and trained Social Worker. She is a graduate of Texas Woman's University and Southern Methodist University Graduate School of Public Administration. Sue's husband Henry is the past Director of the City of Dallas Day Resource Center for the Homeless. They have three children and have lived in Plano, Texas for over twenty years.

Sue L. Adkins

ISBN 0-9672605-9-0
Cheudi Publishing Plano, Texas 75094-0572

www.ingramcontent.com/pod-product-compliance
Lightning Source LLC
Chambersburg PA
CBHW051830090426
42736CB00011B/1733